Bar Mitzvah, Bat Mitzvah

Bar Mitzvah, Bat Mitzvah

How Jewish Boys & Girls Come of Age

by Bert Metter

illustrated by Marvin Friedman

Clarion Books
Ticknor & Fields: a Houghton Mifflin Company
New York

The author would like to thank Rabbi Robert Rothman of Community Synagogue, Rye, New York, Rabbi Hillel Silverman of Temple Sholom, Greenwich, Connecticut, and Rabbi Lynne Landsberg of Central Synagogue, New York, New York for reading and commenting on the manuscript.

The illustrator would like to acknowledge the wonderful and exuberant cooperation of Rabbi Fredric Kazan of Temple Adath Israel in Merion, Pennsylvania.

Clarion Books
Ticknor & Fields, a Houghton Mifflin Company
Text copyright © 1984 by Bert Metter
Illustrations copyright © 1984 by Marvin Friedman

Library of Congress Cataloging in Publication Data

Metter, Bert.
Bar mitzvah, bat mitzvah.
Includes index.
Summary: Describes the Jewish ceremonies of bar and bat mitzvah with a discussion of their history and the effect they have had on the lives of those who have experienced them.
1. Bar mitzvah—Juvenile literature. 2. Bat mitzvah —Juvenile literature. [1. Bar mitzvah. 2. Bat mitzvah] I. Friedman, Marvin, ill. II. Title.
BM707.M45 1984   296.4'424   83-23230
RNF ISBN 0–89919–149–5
PAP ISBN 0–89919–292–0
Y 10 9 8 7 6 5 4 3 2 1

New Hanover County Public Library
Northeast Branch

Requested Slip

Author: Metter, Bert.
Title: Bar mitzvah, bat mitzvah : how
  Jewish boys & girls come of age / by
  Bert Metter ; illustrated by Marvin
Call Number:
Units:
Copy Number: 1
Item Barcode: 34200001242045
Logon Location: Northeast Regional
Request Expiration Date: 8/31/2005
PATRON NAME: Carey, Rebecca S.
Patron Barcode: 24200100109016
Patron Address:
  3910 Wrightsville Ave.
  Wilmington, NC 28403
Patron Phone: 910-792-0048
Pickup Location: Northeast Regional
Check In Date: 9/1/2004 9:09:57 AM
Restrictions:

Have a nice day!

*For my wife, Roslyn, who helped pilot my family
through three bar mitzvah ceremonies.*

*Torah scroll with crown
and cover*

Contents

1. Your Day

You go to bed early because the next day is a big day, your bar mitzvah.

But you don't go to sleep right away because you are thinking about a lot of things.

You lie in bed, and in your mind you go over the prayers that you are to read tomorrow. And you recite the speech you will have to give.

The rabbi said you are going to do just fine. Your parents said you are going to do just fine. Everybody said you are going to do just fine.

Or maybe they think you *aren't* going to do just fine. Maybe they only want you to feel good. They probably tell all the kids they're going to do just fine.

You are up early.

And you arrive at the temple early.

The rabbi talks to you for a few minutes—words of encouragement.

Then you go into the sanctuary with your mother and father.

Soon it is crowded.

You see faces you know. Aunts. Uncles. Cousins. Friends. The whole world is there.

You sit quietly and try to relax.

The service begins. The sound of talking changes to the sound of prayers.

The rabbi and the congregation pray. The rabbi reads. The congregation responds. Back and forth. Rabbi. Congregation. Rabbi. Congregation. You can feel the rhythm of the service. The cantor sings. The choir sings. The pages of the prayer book turn and the service flows.

Now the rabbi turns and walks to the ark, where the Torah scrolls are kept. The curtains are pulled open, and the rabbi carefully lifts the Torah scrolls out—the scrolls with their words from the Bible. Now your relatives are called up, one by one—honored—to recite Torah blessings.

Then it is your turn.

You walk to the lectern.

And now it is not the rabbi leading the congregation in prayer, not your relatives praying, not the cantor singing. It is you.

And every eye is on you.

You don't concentrate on the faces, but on the prayers.

You recite a blessing. Then you read your passages from the Torah, the Bible passages, the words you have been studying. It is quiet, but you don't notice.

Then that part is over. You have done it. You have

stood as an adult and prayed in front of the congregation.

Your father then says his special prayer. He gives thanks for your moral graduation. In a religious sense, you are now responsible for yourself. An obligation has passed from your father to you.

And then it is time for your speech.

You look at the congregation, at all the people watching you.

And you begin. The words you have worked on you say once more. You give your comments on your passage

from the Torah and your feelings about what this day means to you.

And then that is over.

You sit on the side as the service continues.

Finally the congregation rises, and you walk with the rabbi to the ark to return the Torah scrolls to their place.

The rabbi turns to you and welcomes you now as a *bar mitzvah*, a son of the commandment, a full member of the congregation.

You help the rabbi close the curtains that cover the ark.

The choir sings the closing hymns.

The service is over.

You are a bar mitzvah.

You stand in the receiving line with your parents. There is enough handshaking and kissing to last you a thousand years.

And then it is time for the celebration. The party. Food. Gifts. Music. Fun.

That night you don't go to bed very early.

But you go to bed very tired.

And, somehow, you feel more than just a day older.

2. How the Day Came to Be

BAR mitzvah. Bat mitzvah.
How did they begin?

Why are they done the way they are done?

Down through history, many groups of people have had rituals to mark the time when a boy becomes a man —and a girl becomes a woman.

Bar mitzvah, which means "son of the commandment," and bat mitzvah, which means "daughter of the commandment," are the ways the Jewish people mark the coming of age of their children.

It is the time when a child becomes responsible for following the rules of Jewish life—the commandments. And it is the time when a child steps up and becomes a full-fledged member of the Jewish community.

But the bar mitzvah ceremony did not come straight from the Bible. It did not always exist as we know it today. It was created to fill a need—it evolved and grew.

Coming-of-age rites go back to a time even before the beginning of the Jewish religion.

Sociologists have recorded the rites of passage of tribes and cultures from all parts of the world. These rites reflected the life and the hopes of the people who practiced them.

Before initiation into a tribe, boys usually had to pass some sort of test. After they had done this, an elaborate ceremony celebrated their coming of age.

The ceremony of the Karimojong, a Ugandan tribe, involved a child in the spearing, cooking, and eating of an ox. This was done in the hope that the child would own many cattle and lead a long life. The rituals of certain ancient tribes of central North America revolved around strength in warfare. For example, boys might have to drag heavy weights attached to their chests or legs.

In the interior of British Columbia, tribal ceremonies related to future occupations. Boys rolled stones downhill and raced them to the bottom, hoping to grow into fleet-footed warriors. Girls dropped stones inside their dresses so that their babies would be born as easily as a pebble drops to the ground.

Historians tell us that in ancient times it was most common for boys to be initiated into a tribe between the ages of twelve and fourteen.

This was natural. It is the time a boy usually reaches sexual maturity. His voice gets deeper, and hair begins to grow on his face. He begins to become manly.

When Jewish history began, initiation ceremonies like these were probably common. But the Jewish people changed the emphasis of their coming-of-age rites. The rites became more of a spiritual and less of a physical experience.

Ancient Jewish law set twenty as one key age of maturity. That was when a man was expected to pay taxes or to go to fight if there was a war.

But for other purposes, the rabbis fixed the age of responsibility at thirteen for boys and twelve for girls— since girls usually mature about a year earlier.

Those were the "turning point" ages.

But in those days, being a child was different than it is today. In many ways children moved through life at a much faster pace.

Being young did not last as long as it does now.

The custom then was for children to begin studying the Bible when they first learned to read—as early as five years old. They worked earlier. Sometimes they were married by the time they were fifteen.

Many children were advanced enough in their religious studies to take part in services—to come of age— before they became thirteen. And that was fine. There was no rule or custom to hold them back.

In fact, they were encouraged. The younger the better.

They were expected to live up to the commandments as soon as they could understand them.

But thirteen was the official age. By then it became a young person's *duty* to follow the commandments.

By thirteen a boy's vow was considered a valid vow— and he was held to it.

By thirteen his word became acceptable in a court of law.

By thirteen he was expected to fast on the Jewish Day

of Atonement—Yom Kippur—just as an adult was expected to do.

When he was thirteen, a boy was brought to an elder rabbi of the community. The rabbi blessed him and prayed that he would follow the commandments and do good deeds. That was all.

There was no bar mitzvah ceremony as we know it. Many children younger than thirteen had already been

European Torah scholars

taking part in services for years. There was no need for a ceremony.

But in the Middle Ages, about seven hundred years ago, some Jewish communities in Northern Europe changed their attitude about very young children taking part in services.

It was felt that before the age of thirteen a boy was too young to take an adult role in religious ceremonies—too young really to understand what was happening.

The practice of very young children participating in services was discouraged.

Gradually the custom of waiting until a boy was thirteen became accepted. And with this acceptance a thirteenth birthday became a more important occasion.

The occasion seemed to call for some sort of special ceremony.

And so a ceremony was created.

Gradually this ceremony grew more important and more elaborate. It grew into the kind of bar mitzvah ceremony we have today. And it was followed, much later, by a somewhat similar bat mitzvah ceremony for girls.

בָּרוּךְ אַתָּה

יְיָ אֱלֹהֵינוּ

מֶלֶךְ

הָעוֹלָם אֲשֶׁר

קִדְּשָׁנוּ בְּמִצְוֹתָיו

וְצִוָּנוּ לְהַדְלִיק

נֵר שֶׁל שַׁבָּת

3. The Day for Girls

IN biblical times—and down through history—women played a far different role in life than they do today.

For the first time in the United States there are now more women working outside the home than working full time at raising children and running a household.

Women work as police officers and army officers. Women repair telephone lines and ride race horses. Women are doctors, lawyers, business leaders.

Once these jobs were for men only.

Things have changed.

Women's role in religion is also changing.

Traditionally, Jewish women did not take the same part in prayer services as men did. Women played a separate, less active role. Their main role was in the home, not the synagogue.

A woman lights the Sabbath candles in the home.

At one time all synagogues had separate sections for women. They sat apart, sometimes on balconies.

At a bar mitzvah ceremony, women would throw

candy down as part of the celebration when a boy finished his Torah reading.

Women still sit apart today in Orthodox congregations.

In other branches of the Jewish religion, such as Conservative and Reform Judaism, women and men sit together.

In these congregations, the woman's role no longer differs as much from the man's as it did in the past.

Over the years, as the bar mitzvah ceremony became popular in Europe, a coming-of-age ceremony for girls also developed.

It originated in France and Italy about two hundred years ago and gradually spread to other countries.

At twelve a girl would become bat (or bas) mitzvah—a daughter of the commandment. (*Bat* and *bas* are written identically in Hebrew.)

Girls came of age before boys because they came of age physically sooner than boys.

Scholars said the age of thirteen for boys mentioned in ancient Jewish writing could be interpreted as meaning twelve for girls.

The bat mitzvah ceremony was introduced in the United States in 1922.

It is now a part of Jewish religious life in most Conservative and Reform congregations in Europe, Israel, South America, the United States—throughout much of the world.

The form of the ceremony varies by congregation. In many congregations it is essentially the same as the bar mitzvah ceremony for boys.

4. The Ceremony

THE bar mitzvah ceremony did not come about because it was ordained by religious leaders.

It was not planned.

The bar mitzvah ceremony grew because people in certain communities in Germany and France felt a need for it.

It grew out of past traditions into a new tradition. Gradually it became accepted in many Northern European congregations, and over the years it spread south to other countries.

New customs did not usually spread from one Jewish community to another or from one country to another. Each area had its own special tastes, its own preferences.

But the bar mitzvah ceremony overcame local pride and habit. It became a part of Jewish life around the world. It was like a new flower that somehow spread and took root and grew in many different climates.

Just what is involved in the ceremony?

There are the scrolls on which the essence of Jewish law —the Teaching— is inscribed.

There is the "going up" of the youngster to the Teaching.

There is the parents' prayer of thanks and the youngster's traditional speech. And there is often a celebration meal afterward. Let's look at each of these.

The Teaching

On three days of the week—Monday, Thursday, Saturday—Jewish prayer services focus on the first section of the Bible. The bar mitzvah ceremony can take place on any one of these days. And it focuses on this same section of the Bible. For this section—the first five books, called the Books of Moses—are the heart of the Jewish religion.

Jews call these books the Teaching. The Hebrew word is *Torah*.

The Torah has influenced a great part of the human race. In the Christian religion, these books are considered holy and are part of the Christian Old Testament.

The Torah is considered holy in the Islamic religion, too.

But the relationship of these five books to the Jewish people is special.

These books tell the story of creation: "In the beginning God created the heaven and the earth...." They tell of the birth of the Jewish people—the agreement, called the covenant, between God and Abraham: "Obey Me and I will protect you."

ABOVE: *Torah crown*
RIGHT: *The scrolls are wound around wooden holders called "trees of life."*

18

They include the laying down of the Ten Commandments: the essence of Jewish belief, the written law.

They conclude with the death of Moses.

A bar mitzvah ceremony marks a new stage in the relationship between a child and these sacred Jewish books. The child is now personally responsible for living up to the Teaching.

The Scrolls and the Ark

Every synagogue has Bibles that include the Torah. But every synagogue also contains Torah scrolls. They are

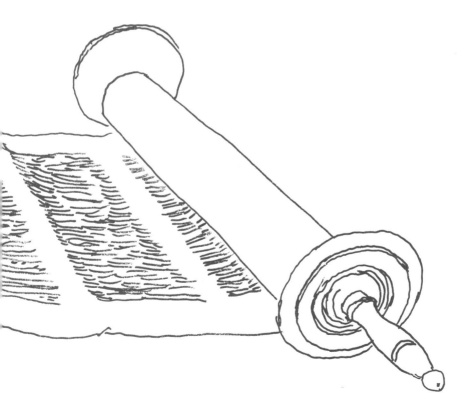

special copies of the Teaching, handwritten by scribes on parchment.

The scrolls are usually kept at the front of the congregation, in an enclosure called the ark.

The scrolls and the ark go back to the beginning of Jewish history. In biblical times, the ark was a portable chest. The Bible tells how the commandments received by Moses from God were inscribed on tablets of stone. The tablets were carried in the ark by the Jews as they marched from Egypt searching for a homeland.

The ark with the commandments led the procession, like a flag. It showed who the Jews were: they were the people who carried God's word. This made them feel strong and protected by God.

Each day when they lifted the ark to start to march or put it down when they came to rest, Moses said a special prayer.

When the Jews had settled in Jerusalem and temples were built, the ark containing the commandments was kept indoors.

Eventually it became the custom to build an ark for the Torah permanently into the eastern wall of every synagogue.

And that's where we see the ark today.

The ark with the Torah scrolls stands at the architectural center of the synagogue.

It is built so that when we face it, we look to Jerusalem, the site of the first Jewish Temple.

There are usually ceremonial curtains draped around it and a light that never goes out hung above it.

The scrolls are treated with the greatest respect. When

they are removed from the ark, or returned to it, the congregation stands. When the ark is opened or closed, the prayers of Moses are chanted. These are the prayers Moses said when the ark was carried forward or put down at rest on the march from Egypt.

The bar mitzvah ceremony calls a youngster up to the ark and the scrolls of the Teaching—and new responsibility.

Going Up

The scrolls of the Torah—the Teaching—are not meant to be lifeless symbols. The Torah is the center around which Jewish life revolves. It is meant to be read, absorbed, used as a guide to life.

And it *is* read. The Torah is divided up so that during fifty-two weeks of services, the entire Torah is read through once.

The readings proceed like the seasons of the year and mark off all the holidays.

Each year at the end of the cycle there is a celebration, and the scrolls are paraded through the synagogue.

At the bar mitzvah service, as at every service, the scrolls are removed from the ark and placed on a stand for reading.

Before the reading, special blessings are given:

> Blessed art Thou, O Lord, our God,
> King of the Universe,
> Who has chosen us from all people
> and given us Thy Law. . . .

21

אנכי ••
לא יהיה
לא תשא
זכור את
כבד את

*Torah scrolls in a 16th-
century ark from Mantua,
Italy*

An ark from an 18th-century Dutch synagogue

Members of the congregation are traditionally honored by being called up to recite these blessings.

This honor is called an *aliyah* in Hebrew—a "going up."

An *aliyah* can be used to mark many special occasions.

You may be called up before or after your marriage.

You may be called up after the birth of a child.

And you are called up to mark your coming of age at a bar or bat mitzvah ceremony.

The custom at a Saturday morning service is for seven members of the congregation to be called on to recite blessings.

The father of the child is called up. In some congregations, both parents are called up.

And so are other close relatives.

When you are called up to the Torah scrolls for the first time, you are making a spiritual ascent.

You are being called up to become a member of the congregation.

Responsible. Accountable. A participant.

On the day of the bar or bat mitzvah ceremony you take part in the service as never before. That part may be large or small. It depends on the custom of your congregation and on your ability and ambition.

You read a blessing before and after the Torah readings.

You read part—or all—of that day's portion of the Teaching.

Other parts of the Bible are also read from at the service.

You may chant some or all of these.

The chanting follows an ancient melody. Words in certain sections of the Hebrew Bible have accent markings. These markings relate to musical notes. They tell how the words are to be chanted. The chantings punctuate the sentences and help make their meaning clear.

Whether your part is large or small, the ceremony brings you into the service and into the congregation—as an adult.

A Day for Your Parents

Traditionally, there is a special prayer said at the bar and bat mitzvah ceremony by the father of the child or by both parents.

Up until your thirteenth year if you are a boy, or your twelfth if you are a girl, your parents are responsible for your sins.

Your slate is, theoretically, clean.

Up until this time, as a child, you may not have understood the difference between right and wrong.

But this is the day you accept responsibility.

You become a son or daughter of the commandment.

And for this your parent gives thanks.

The parent's prayer goes back to the days before bar mitzvah ceremonies began. It was said when a father brought his child to a rabbi in the community to be blessed when the child turned thirteen.

It is a simple prayer:

> Blessed be Thou, O Lord, our God,
> King of the Universe,
> Who has relieved me from responsibility
> for my child. . . .

This is, of course, not a parent expressing relief at getting off the hook. It is an expression of happiness that a child is ready to enter the religious community. Now, at last, the child is ready to accept responsibility for following the commandments or laws that govern Jewish life.

But the Jewish religion is family–minded. The obligation of the parents to guide a child continues. And the obligation of the child to the parent never ends, as the commandments make clear: "Honor your father and your mother. . . ."

The Jewish religion is also practical. It teaches that parents prepare their children for accepting new responsibilities.

For example, once past bar or bat mitzvah age, a youngster is expected to fast a full day on Yom Kippur, the Day of Atonement. But traditionally, the parents would have started a child fasting a few hours a day on each Yom Kippur from the time the child was nine or ten.

A Day to Express Yourself

Most of a bar or bat mitzvah ceremony is designed to bring you into the flow of the ceremony.

You blend in.

You are being absorbed into the congregation.

But there is also a part of the ceremony in which you express yourself as an individual—your speech.

Traditionally there is a short discourse—the Hebrew name is *dereshah*—in which you comment on what your bar or bat mitzvah day means to you.

The speech is prepared with guidance from a religious teacher, rabbi, or parent.

Your speech may be related to the portion of the Teaching you read at the service. It may also express your feelings as you step over the threshold to religious maturity.

While the ceremony usually follows the beaten path of tradition, your speech allows some originality. It can bear your stamp.

The practice of commenting on and explaining parts of

the Torah goes back to the beginnings of the Jewish religion.

While the first five books of the Bible are the core of Jewish belief, around that core are other sections of the Bible and other writings, commentaries that became accepted as holy over the centuries.

OPPOSITE: *Working with the rabbi in his study*
BELOW: *Composing the speech*

From ancient times, preachers would take a biblical verse and elaborate on it. The tradition of commenting on the Scriptures guided the growth of Jewish sacred writings.

But this is the work of prophets, rabbis, and scholars.

Where do twelve- or thirteen-year-old children come in?

The answer takes us back hundreds of years to the days of the Crusades.

Great changes swept across Europe.

Jews had generally been free to live where they pleased, to travel, to work at any job.

But religious and political wars forced them into "Jewish-only" sections called ghettos.

Restricted to the ghettos, kept from outside activities, European Jews turned to religious study more intensely than ever.

For the children, there were few diversions.

There was no TV, no radio, no movies, no magazines, no vacation trips.

There were no public schools.

But there were religious schools. And plenty of religious study.

By the time children reached thirteen or so, they were often skilled in commenting on portions of the Bible.

The brightest were like scholarly lawyers who could make a case for or against the meaning of a biblical passage.

And so the custom grew for them to display their talent

Studying for a bat mitzvah

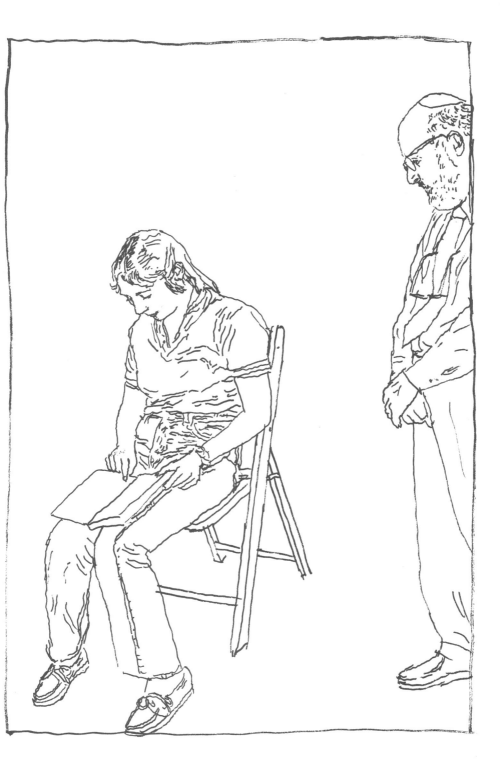

by giving a discourse, a speech, on the portion of the Teaching read at their bar mitzvah service. This was often done at a reception in their home after morning services. And it could be a grand event. Relatives, neighbors, and friends would be invited to hear the lecture by the new child of the commandment.

Then, about three hundred years ago, new political upheavals came to Europe, climaxing in the French Revolution. Ghetto walls came down. Freedom of movement returned. Jews reentered the mainstream. They traveled, chose their work, mixed with other people.

As life became more open, religious study grew less intense.

And the speeches at bar mitzvah ceremonies gradually became less long and less learned.

Yet the tradition of the speech continues to our own time. Usually the youngster thanks parents and teachers who have provided guidance. And he or she expresses hopes that the lessons of the Torah will be applied wisely in the years of maturity ahead.

After your speech, the rabbi will usually say a few words to you.

He will bless you.

And he prays that you will follow the commandments and serve God.

Finally, the scrolls are returned. The ark is closed. The prayers have all been said. The service ends, having gone like most other services.

But at this one, you passed a milestone.

And now it's time to celebrate.

A Day to Celebrate

The tradition of a special meal to celebrate the coming of age of a Jewish youngster goes back to the days when the bar mitzvah ceremony first took shape.

Relatives would have been invited to the services at the synagogue. Neighbors and friends were often present. It was natural that people wanted to stay together afterward to eat and discuss the big day.

And a dinner gave youngsters the place and the audience to display their knowledge of the Teaching with a speech.

Today, the custom of hospitality after a bar mitzvah ceremony is satisfied in many ways.

It can be as simple as bread, wine, and honey cake in a room at the synagogue.

It can be a meal at home or at a restaurant.

Or it can be more.

Much more.

Dazzling and elaborate affairs have been held. People like to have a good time. It's all very human.

But sometimes it's not all very religious.

Ever since biblical days, rabbis have struggled with the problem of the overdone celebration. Occasional excesses have not been limited to bar mitzvah celebrations.

Religious laws were created, called sumptuary regulations, to keep the lid on.

For one thing, the rabbis pointed out that excesses were not right spiritually. For another, Jews were a minority in most communities. They didn't want to stir up

A new bar mitzvah celebrates with his relatives and friends.

unnecessary envy or anger among their non-Jewish neighbors.

In Italy, about five hundred years ago, rabbis ruled that there would be a tax on every guest over a fixed limit. To keep taxes down, your guest list had to be held down.

In Poland there was a decree that limited the jewelry

that could be worn: two rings on weekdays, four on weekends, six on holidays.

At one time or another there were restrictions on what kind of clothing could be worn, how many courses could be served, what kind of gifts could be given at weddings.

All these rules were to keep celebrations within bounds.

The rabbis felt that a party marking a religious event should retain a religious spirit.

And that's still the feeling today, whether there is a small reception within a synagogue or a large affair anywhere else.

5. What the Day Changes

BECOMING bar mitzvah—a child of the commandment—brings new duties and privileges.

First, of course, you are morally responsible for living according to the commandments.

And you are counted as an adult in religious matters.

For example, in order for community prayer services to be held, at least ten men must be present. Ten makes up the required minimum. (The Hebrew word is *minyan*.) Once a boy turns thirteen, he may be counted as one of the men.

And, in tradition-minded Jewish congregations, the bar mitzvah ceremony marks a change in weekday prayer. As an adult, a boy may now wear the traditional prayer shawl, called a *tallit*.

These shawls are descended from the robes worn by rabbis in ancient times. They have rows of fringes at either end as reminders of the many commandments to be followed.

ABOVE: *Learning to put on the* TALLIT *and the* TEFILLIN
OPPOSITE: TEFILLIN *are kept in a cloth bag.*

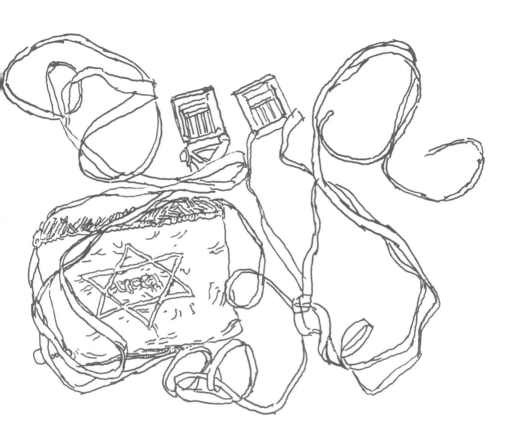

Along with the shawl, a boy would now also wear *tefil-lin*—tiny pieces of parchment with Torah prayers written on them, held within two small leather cases. These cases are wrapped around the arm and the forehead with leather straps. This practice is based on a passage in the Bible that says the commandments are to be bound as a sign on your arm and worn as frontlets between your eyes.

6. The Day Takes Many Forms

JEWS are a diverse people.

Jews live in many countries.

Jews don't dress alike, talk alike, live alike.

On the streets of New York or London or Tel Aviv two men pass each other. One has a wide-brimmed black hat, a long black coat, a full beard and braided sideburns. The other is clean-shaven and wears a three-piece business suit and aviator-style glasses.

Both are Jews.

That's why there is no such thing as a universal bar or bat mitzvah ceremony—exactly the same everywhere, in all details.

In Great Britain, the father of the child often wears a top hat. And the child may have to pass a standardized

Trying on grandfather's TALLIT

written examination in Jewish knowledge and Hebrew before being accepted for the bar mitzvah ceremony.

At some Oriental synagogues, the ceremony includes the first wearing of the prayer shawl and wrapping of the *tefillin* around the arm and head for praying.

In some Orthodox Moroccan synagogues, you can hear

A bar mitzvah in London, England

the women wailing in their separate upper gallery as they shower nuts and raisins down upon the child when he finishes his Torah readings.

At one Israeli kibbutz (a working farm community), boys and girls are sent out to undergo a tough camping expedition as part of the experience of coming of age.

Some Jewish families travel thousands of miles from their homes to hold a bar or bat mitzvah ceremony in front of the ancient Western Wall in Jerusalem, site of the First Temple.

Others may prefer to hold the ceremony at a quiet rustic retreat, close to home.

In recent years a custom has developed in which those past thirteen have had bar or bat mitzvah ceremonies.

Sometimes, they have been far past thirteen.

In June 1981, seven women ranging in age from eighty-one to ninety-nine held a joint bat mitzvah ceremony at a New Jersey home for the aged.

In February 1981, a West Point cadet, who had missed the ceremony at thirteen, had it at twenty-one in Eisenhower Hall at the Military Academy.

This is not done to follow Jewish law. You are bound to the commandments once you reach twelve or thirteen, even if you have not had a formal ceremony.

It is done to express your belief in the commandments. Or it is done to capture an experience you feel you missed and want to have.

As people's needs vary in different times and different parts of the world, the ceremony may vary.

But the essentials have stayed the same.

7. A Day to Remember

WHAT sort of personal experience is a bar or bat mitzvah ceremony?

In years to come, how will you feel about it? What will you remember?

We asked some prominent Jewish people to think back.

Jacob Javitz, who served four terms as a United States senator from New York, recollects a day in 1922:

> I remember standing in our railroad flat on the Lower East Side of New York on a Saturday after synagogue services and making my bar mitzvah speech. The guests were mostly relatives. And a few friends. Probably thirty people in all. When everyone had left and I was alone again, I felt I had really accomplished something. I felt I had become a man.

At the end of a bat mitzvah day

Mayor Ed Koch of New York City remembers growing up in New Jersey and the ceremony at a temple in High Street in Newark:

> It was an exciting day and well attended by members of my family, including about fifty relatives. We were poor, so the party was held in our apartment, but it was a wonderful occasion and I look back on it with fond memories.

Abraham Goldstein, former dean of the Yale Law School, remembers being slightly worried about getting up in front of the congregation. But he remembers feeling relaxed while reciting his prayers. And he felt a sense of accomplishment when it was over.

Milton Friedman, winner of the 1976 Nobel Prize in Economics, remembers looking confidently forward to the day of his bar mitzvah. He felt calm, and everything went smoothly.

Red Holzman, who coached the New York Knickerbockers to the world basketball championship in 1970, remembers his bar mitzvah ceremony as an important personal experience, performed in a quiet, simple manner.

Jan Peerce, an opera star whose tenor voice has been featured at the Metropolitan and other great opera houses, recalls:

> I remember vividly my parents did not care for me to make any kind of ordinary speech. Instead, being a singer with a good thirteen-year-old alto voice, I studied and prepared myself to be the cantor (prayer

singer) in our little synagogue. I sang the service, and it left a lasting impression on me...and seemed to impress some listeners, too.

Gene Wilder, comedian and actor, (*Young Frankenstein, Blazing Saddles*) remembers feeling the usual nervousness beforehand and the usual relief afterward. He is critical of some bar mitzvah ceremonies he sees these days which focus on the parents rather than the child—and which are more festive than religious.

Judith Kaplan Eisenstein remembers her bat mitzvah ceremony because of the stir it caused. On May 6, 1922, Judith, then twelve and a half, became the first girl in the United States to have a bat mitzvah ceremony. Judith's father, Rabbi Mordecai Kaplan, was founder of the Reconstructionist movement, a branch of Conservative Judaism. She recalls:

> My bat mitzvah ceremony attracted not only the whole congregation, but many spectators. It received much attention, and I felt a great sense of pride.

Beverly Sills, one of the world's leading operatic sopranos, did not have a bat mitzvah. It is only in recent years that the ceremony for girls has become more common. She says, "My two brothers had bar mitzvah ceremonies, but when it came to the girl in the family, it did not seem necessary. The rule in my family was: 'The boys will be smart and go to college. The girl will be an opera singer.'"

Theodore Bikel, folk singer and actor, had his bar mitzvah ceremony in Europe, where he lived as a child. He remembers giving his speech in Hebrew. And he remembers the dedication to learning:

> Over there, learning is emphasized. There is less insistence that "the kid get it right" and more on understanding the words. The child is far more at the center of attention.

Harry Henschel, president of the Bulova Watch Company, remembers the rabbi who stood with him at his bar mitzvah ceremony fifty years ago. Sixteen years later, the same rabbi officiated at Harry Henschel's wedding.

Frederic Dannay, creator of Ellery Queen and co-author of more than forty Ellery Queen mysteries, remembered his ceremony, his speech, and the party at his home. But, as a writer, he recalled one gift with special fondness:

> I received a set of books by James Fenimore Cooper— five volumes bound in smooth red leather, with gold decorative stamping. I have taken them with me in moves all over the country. Today, more than sixty years after my bar mitzvah, that set of books is still sitting on one of my bookshelves. Only a short time ago the gold stamping began to fade.

Sol Linowitz, former United States ambassador and chairman of the board of Xerox Corporation, remembers his ceremony clearly:

I believe the bar mitzvah ceremony should be a solemn and memorable occasion, highlighting the spiritual aspects. Mine was, and I'm grateful.

The day of your bar mitzvah or bat mitzvah ceremony is likely to stay with you for a long time.

8. A Unique Day

OF all Jewish rituals, the bar mitzvah and bat mitzvah ceremonies have grown especially popular and more elaborate over the years.

Why?

Taking part in the ceremony doesn't make you Jewish.

Children born of a Jewish mother are considered Jewish.

Males enter the Jewish covenant with God by being circumcised when they are eight days old.

And you automatically become responsible for obeying the commandments when you are a boy of thirteen or a girl of twelve. This is so whether or not you have a bar or bat mitzvah ceremony.

Yet the ceremony has filled a need. It has evolved, spread throughout the world, grown stronger.

For it is a time when you stand up on your own in front of your family, your friends, and your congregation and accept the Jewish Teaching.

In modern life, religion plays a less visible and less dominant role for many people than it did in the past. And that may be why standing up and affirming your faith seems important and has grown in popularity.

The ceremony is valuable for other reasons, too.

As children grow, they begin to face moral questions. The religious study encouraged by and required for the ceremony helps prepare them for facing these questions.

And, in a way, a bar or bat mitzvah ceremony sets a pattern for meeting many of life's challenges.

You prepare yourself—as you do when studying for the ceremony.

You take a deep breath, stand up, and do the job—as you do at the service.

And, when you're lucky, you enjoy your accomplishment—as you do at the celebration meal.

That's when you can say, "I did it."

Congratulations.

You're on your way.

Index